D1336384

household management for men

First published in Great Britain in 2004 by
Cassell Illustrated, a division of
Octopus Publishing Group Ltd
2-4 Heron Quays
London
E14 4JP

A CIP catalogue record for this book is
available from the British Library.

ISBN 1-84403274-4
9781844032747

Conceived, designed and produced by
Quid Publishing
Fourth Floor
Sheridan House
112-116A Western Road
Hove BN3 1DD
England
www.quidpublishing.com

Publisher: Nigel Browning
Publishing Manager: Sophie Martin
Author: Jane Moseley
Project Management: Essential Works
Illustrations: Matt Pagett

Printed and bound in China by
Midas Printing International Ltd

NOTE
Every effort has been taken to ensure that
all information in this book is correct and
compatible with national standards at the
time of publication. This book is not
intended to replace manufacturers'
instructions in the use of their tools or
products – always follow their safety
guidelines.

The author, publisher and copyright
holder assume no responsibility for any
injury, loss or damage caused or sustained
as a consequence of the use and
application of the contents of this book.

A LITTLE BOOK OF DOMESTIC WISDOM

bathroom

household management for

men

Contents

Bathroom

'The bathroom is a waterproof stage on which to strut your stuff. Clean up your act and you may win a BAFCA (Bathroom Award For Clean Acts).'
JOANNA RAMPLEY-STURGEON

The Art and Science of Domestic Wisdom

Let's start with a few little-known but interesting facts. Household management is both a science and an art; it uses both sides of the male brain and is a practical and spiritual exercise – practical because it establishes order, hygiene and safety within the home environment; spiritual because it makes you feel more comfortable and secure within your own four walls (plus rather pleased with yourself). Even better, housework is also an aerobic exercise that allows you to flex your muscles and push your weight about at home without annoying people.

Housework is not dull, boring or a waste of leisure hours that could be better spent in front of a television or at the bar. It saves time, creates order out of chaos, burns calories and makes you sexier. Are you more interested now? Read on.

Men, when questioned about how much housework they do, often reply: 'Not my department,' 'Far too busy at work,' 'What's the point? It always looks the same five minutes later,' and 'Do you reckon Hercules did the dusting?' However, in our fast-changing world, increasing numbers of men share the household chores or, indeed, assume full responsibility for them. The dynamics are changing. Real men do housework – it's a fact. And real men get rewards.

This *Little Book of Domestic Wisdom* demonstrates how to approach household tasks positively and effectively, how to schedule, organize and execute tasks

efficiently – just like any other job that lands in the daily in-tray – and shows how to enjoy a similar sense of achievement and fulfillment. Some jobs are more rewarding than others: dusty surfaces can stare you in the face for some time without any major repercussions, but neglecting the bath, basin or the laundry basket will lead to instant inconvenience and hygiene hazards. However, just think how great you feel when the filing tray is empty. It's the same with housework. And you haven't got the journey home afterwards.

What to do when

Don't let the very thought of housework overwhelm you, just like a huge work project upon which you cannot get started. Ease yourself into it and do a little each day. Don't wait until things get completely out of control before tackling them – tasks will take twice the amount of time and be half as effective. To do it properly you need a system, a routine and a schedule. 'Diarize, prioritize, realize' is a good mission statement – it works just as well at home as on the time management course and in the office.

First things first

Individuals should assume responsibility for their own clutter. Taking ownership of a problem is half way to solving it. Admitting to ownership of a pair of odorous socks on the bathroom floor is the first step on the road to removing, washing, folding and finding them a good home. Don't upset people by de-junking their possessions without consultation. It would be like reading their post and dumping it without their knowledge or consent. Set a time schedule for the 'house de-junk' and stick to it.

If some tasks are going to take more than a few days (eg removing all evidence of mould and mildew from the bathroom walls and ceiling) you will need to come up with a few long-term goals rather than immediate ones.

A little every day goes a long way

You will feel so much better when you get up in the morning if you are faced with a clean basin and bath, a hygienic loo and if you have already sorted out your laundry. Equally, on returning from a hard day's work at the office or in the library, the feel-good factor for you and your housemates or partner goes up dramatically if the bathroom is welcoming and savoury. You might have to get ready for a hot date quickly. Do you really want to have to battle through debris to get in the shower?

Mess attracts mess – it's a fact. A lonely and unwashed sock is quickly joined by three potential mates – they reproduce easily and soon you have a little family. If someone else can leave clothes unwashed, why can't you? Hold on a minute, though – what if someone pops round unannounced – your boss, friend or potential romantic interest perhaps? How impressed would they be to find the bathroom in a total mess? Your bathroom reflects your attitude to hygiene. If you are a slob at home, you may well be at work. Think clean thoughts and put them into action. Domestic God and domestic hygiene go hand in hand into a sunlit, romantic horizon.

THE END

How To Use This Book

This book is aimed at a fairly wide audience – male students; young and not-so-young working men, whether single, married or in partnerships; stay-at-home men, both novices and experienced home managers; and all the women out there who want to pass on the art of household management to their menfolk, whatever their age or previous knowledge. Some readers will be new to household management, others may have a little or even a lot of experience. They can derive some satisfaction from already having a few techniques and tips under their belt. Beginners will soon get the hang of things and move speedily from the nursery slopes to intermediate level. By page 80, all of you will be experts in the art and science of household management and ready to tackle a few off-piste tasks.

The key to understanding the principles of household management is to read, digest and implement the advice in this *Little Book of Domestic Wisdom*. Pass on what you learn, what you achieve, even what you do wrong. People like to hear about successes and failures on the domestic front and thereby imitate or deviate.

Since time began, wisdom has been passed down orally from generation to generation. Cavemen and women sat round the fire and taught their young how to keep the hearth warm, how to barbecue the wildlife and make duvet covers from their fur. Wisdom learnt at one's parents' knee led to the Barbecue Age becoming the Iron Age and then the Modern Age (with a few eras in between). Continue the tradition. Do it subtly, though. Don't drag

Domestic God

Look out for the Domestic God icon if you want to fast-track to the heart of the matter (or that of your partner).

your partner or housemate around the 21st-century cave by their metaphorical loincloths, telling them what to do in a smug, been-there-done-that-ironed-the-dinosaur-T-shirt kind of way. Share your knowledge gently. Share the housework, too (see page 70). Don't fight over it – buy them a copy for their birthday.

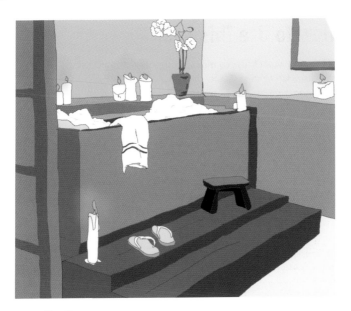

Rewarding Times

We all need to feel congratulated or pampered from time to time, particularly when we have faced a challenge and successfully tackled it. Make sure you reward yourself (if nobody else is going to do it for you) by patting yourself metaphorically on the back and treating yourself to something that makes you feel good – a new book, CD or DVD, a massage, or a bottle of good wine. Tell someone what you've done. You are feeling better already.

Dirty Devil

 Keep an eye out for the Dirty Devil as a warning not to go there, do this, think that, or even suggest the other.

Know Your ...

Bathroom

Strange that in what is often the smallest room in the house, hygiene is the biggest issue. Remember, this is a window on your personal habits, a waterproof stage on which to strut your stuff. Emerge refreshed, rejuvenated and cleaner. No tidemarks, no leftover stubble, no unsavoury clothes or literature. Keep it clean, guys.

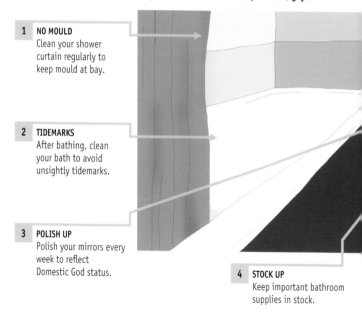

1 NO MOULD
Clean your shower curtain regularly to keep mould at bay.

2 TIDEMARKS
After bathing, clean your bath to avoid unsightly tidemarks.

3 POLISH UP
Polish your mirrors every week to reflect Domestic God status.

4 STOCK UP
Keep important bathroom supplies in stock.

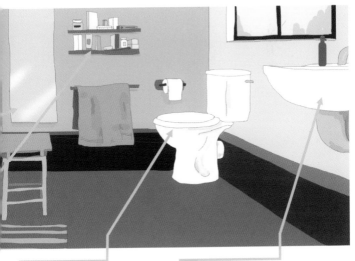

5 KEEP IT CLEAN
Clean the toilet
every day.

6 HYGIENE HARMONY
A brillant basin
is important for
hygiene, health and
household harmony.

Learn, Earn and Burn

Life is all about learning. Domestic life has its very own learning curves, some steeper than others. To scale and conquer, you need to focus. The art of household management can be divided into three key areas: Learn, Earn and Burn.

Three Small Steps for Mankind

1 Learn

Learn the principles of housework – not just the 'what' but the 'why', 'how', 'when' and 'where' involved. It is the first big, important step along the highway to hygiene heaven. This *Little Book of Domestic Wisdom* will explain all these aspects. It will reveal the dangers of not cleaning your home, the secret hazards involved and the risks you are running. It will unravel the mystery of an ancient art made simpler by modern technology. Look what happened when Aladdin tried a spot of polishing on the brass lamp. The same new world could open up to you with just a little effort.

2 Earn

Earn the brownie points and reap the benefits, physical, spiritual and emotional, of mastering what are essentially simple but rewarding (in many senses) techniques. Housework is good for you. It helps keep you hygienic and therefore appealing, it brings with it gold stars and brownie points, and it helps put a new, improved shine on that domestic halo you have been hiding under your dusty bushel all this time. Your romantic, emotional health will get a spring clean.

3 Burn

And, lastly, burn those calories as you master this important art. It is cheaper than going to the gym, it doesn't involve a commute and you kill two birds plus a zillion potential allergens and unpleasant germs with one proverbial stone, swoop of the cloth or flourish of the vacuum. Exercise reduces stress, helps trigger the happy hormones and builds muscle. Housework is indoor exercise. You can choose your own time and your own background music. You are never far from a reviving drink or nourishing snack. What more could you want?

The Whole Equation

Let's look at the whole equation:

Where
DW+S = **D**omestic **W**isdom plus **S**atisfaction

and
hm = household management
w = weekly
d = daily
cb = calories burned
mb = muscle built

$$DW+S = hm\ (w) + 250cb + mb + 1.9\%$$

$$DW+S^2 = hm\ (d) + 500cb + mb + 3.5\%$$

Add to this equation ...

Add to this equation the Domestic God factor and it suddenly starts to add up and make sense. The statistics are even more attractive when you add your potential brownie points (bp) and personal appeal (pa). It is a win-win situation.

Questionnaire

It is time to ask yourself some serious (and some not quite so serious) questions. Have a go at this quick questionnaire to find out just how much you do know about the subject of household management. If you get more

Do You Know It All Already?

How often should you clean the bath?
A) TWICE A WEEK
B) ONCE A MONTH
C) WHEN SOMEONE COMES TO STAY
D) WHEN THERE'S AN 'R' IN THE MONTH
E) DIDN'T KNOW YOU HAD TO

Why light a match in the bathroom?
A) TO LIGHT MY CIGARETTE, SILLY!
B) TO ELIMINATE UNPLEASANT ODOURS
C) TO LIGHT MY CHOCOLATE CIGAR
D) TO LIGHT MY INCENSE STICKS, MAN
E) TO SEE THE LOO IN THE DARK WHEN I HAVE RUN OUT OF BULBS

Do you disinfect your loo brush?
A) EVERY TIME I CLEAN THE LOO
B) YUK – NO
C) NEVER
D) WHEN MY MOTHER COMES
E) I CAN'T – IT MAKES ME ILL

Why is it important to keep the toilet lid down?
A) GIRLS GET CROSS IF YOU DON'T
B) YOUR UNDERWEAR FALLS IN THE PAN OTHERWISE
C) GERMS CAN LEAP OUT WHEN YOU FLUSH
D) SO YOUR PARTNER CAN CHAT TO YOU DURING A SHOWER
E) YOUR DOG MIGHT DRINK THE WATER

Why should you remove dust regularly from surfaces?
A) IT GETS UP YOUR PARTNER'S NOSE
B) THERE IS NEVER ENOUGH TO WRITE YOUR WHOLE NAME IN
C) IT IS FULL OF DEAD DUST MITES AND CAN CAUSE ALLERGIES
D) IT SPOILS THE VIEW ON THE BATHROOM MIRROR
E) YOU DON'T NEED TO – JUST TURN THE LIGHTS DOWN

questions right than wrong, you are weaving your way to wisdom but by no means are you an all-knowing, all-powerful household cleaning agent. If you get more wrong than right, you need this book badly.

When did you last empty the loo bin?
A) LAST WEEK
B) LAST MONTH
C) THIS MORNING
D) DON'T REMEMBER SEEING ONE
E) NEVER

Do you bathe with your dog?
A) NEVER
B) HE GETS IN AFTER ME
C) ON HIS BIRTHDAY
D) SOMETIMES
E) DON'T HAVE A DOG

Look at your bathroom floor. What do you see?
A) A WET TOWEL
B) A CLEAN, EMPTY FLOOR
C) WHAT I WORE YESTERDAY
D) ALL MY UNDERWEAR
E) CAN'T SEE THE FLOOR

How often should you wash your bath mat?
A) WHEN IT IS AS WET AS THE BATH
B) WHEN YOU CAN SMELL IT FROM THE KITCHEN
C) EVERY COUPLE OF MONTHS
D) EVERY WEEK
E) DON'T HAVE ONE. I JUST WET THE CARPET

Why do you need to ventilate the bathroom?
A) TO KEEP MOULD AND MILDEW AT BAY
B) BECAUSE WET TOWELS ON THE FLOOR DRY BETTER
C) TO GET RID OF SMELL OF MY SOCKS DRYING
D) TO GET RID OF SMELL OF MY CIGARETTE
E) MY DOG USES THE BATHROOM TOO

| Technique | Tool | Wisdom | Cleaning | Chore |

Weekly Wonders, Monthly Miracles, Annual Asks

Establishing a routine for chores is important. It's just the same as at the office – a macro and micro analysis. It helps you see the bigger picture. Consider all the jobs that have to be done and create a list or chart that

Chore Chart:

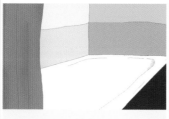

ANNUALLY:
- REMOVE MOULD AND MILDEW FROM CEILINGS AND WALLS (EVERY SIX MONTHS)
- SHAMPOO CARPET

MONTHLY:
- CLEAN FLOOR THOROUGHLY
- POLISH TAPS
- CHECK SUPPLIES OF TOILET PAPER, SHAMPOO AND SOAP
- CLEAN SHOWER CURTAIN (EVERY TWO MONTHS)
- MAKE INVENTORY OF MEDICINE CABINET CONTENTS
- WASH PAINTWORK AND TILES

divides them into four headings: annually, monthly (or quarterly), weekly (or fortnightly if you are very lazy) and daily. Hourly is taking the whole micro stuff just too far... sticking to a weekly schedule really does work.

WEEKLY:
- CLEAN BATH (TWICE A WEEK)
- CHANGE BATH TOWELS (DITTO)
- CLEAN UNIT TOPS
- WASH BATHMAT
- POLISH MIRROR
- VACUUM OR SWEEP FLOOR
- REPLENISH LOO ROLL SUPPLIES

DAILY:
- CLEAN TOILET AND BASIN
- CHECK SUPPLIES
- TRASH THE TRASH
- REPLACE TOILET PAPER
- REMOVE DIRTY LAUNDRY

Technique	Tool	Wisdom	Cleaning	Chore

Domestic God: Top-to-Toe

There is no point making a valiant attempt to keep your home in order if you fail to pay similar attention to your body. Is it not a temple after all? The bathroom is where the cleanse and clear manoeuvres happen.

Top-to-Toe Hygiene Routine

Eyes

Your eyes are the windows to your soul and reflect your habits, particularly the nocturnal ones. Get as much sleep as your body needs rather than as little as your self-imposed routine allows. Eat and drink alcohol in sensible moderation, but drink lots of water to keep hydrated. Reduce puffiness with slices of cucumber. Red equals stop. Don't choose it for your eyes or you will never get the green light in romance.

Nose and Ears

Perversely, hair seems to emigrate from the top of your head and sprout in your nose and ears. Try to keep it under control with nose and hair groomers. Don't use tweezers (ouch) or scissors. Wash in and behind ears regularly and check nose for stalagmites or stalactites, particularly before meeting your new boss or mystery date.

Face

Wash your face morning and night with soap, gel or cleanser. If you have sensitive skin, find a gentle product that suits you. Pay attention to the T-zone (forehead and nose) where skin can be oily and prone to pimples. Remember this is the face you will have for years to come. Wear sunscreen unless you like the craggy look. Exfoliate regularly and moisturize daily. No mixed emotions - lotions and potions are not just for girls.

Hands and Arms

Wash thoroughly and often. Keep soft and supple with hand cream. Make holding hands fun and sensual. How many lobsters do you see arm in arm? Brush nails every day. Dirty fingernails are a no-no. Long ones can be a real turn-off, so trim them weekly.

Regular washing and application of deodorant is the key to maintaining this area. Remember, you have over two million sweat glands. You may want to occasionally trim the region to keep perspiration under control – take care when you do and carry out the process in the shower, not the bedroom.

Body

Keep it clean, toned and moisturized. Skin is the largest organ you have – it protects you from all sorts of nastiness and deserves respect. Exercise strengthens the immune system, so a few stretches and sit-ups and a bit of jogging and general jiggling about will keep you fit and happy. Shower after exercise if you want to have a social life.

Keep your six-pack toned, clean and smooth, and your tummy button free of fluff. It is not a storage solution. No need to dust or vacuum, just wash.

This T-zone must be kept impeccably clean and dry at all times. A large percentage of those sweat glands operate in this area. It's a hygiene-heavy district. Don't share towels at the gym. Change your underwear at least seven times a week (that's every day, by the way).

Wash, moisturise and exercise regularly. You rely on them to get you from A to B. If they send out an SOS, a calf massage in a warm bath will help.

| Technique | Tool | Wisdom | Cleaning | Chore |

A Day in the Life of a Bathroom God

Location, location, location. The bathroom is the hub of human hygiene activity. You will dash in and out in the morning before work and in the evening before a date. You will dive in before bed to prepare for the night ahead. At weekends,

Domestic God's Bathroom Routine

6.30-7am

THE EARLY BIRD
Why not try to get up a bit earlier so that the early morning 'ablutine' (ablution routine) is a more relaxed affair. What you lose on the sleep stakes you gain by winning the race in a clean sweep.

7.02am

KILL TWO BIRDS
Destination – bathroom. ETA – 7am. Stop – have you opened your bedroom window and pulled back the sheet or duvet to air the room and bed? Not applicable if your partner is still in there of course...

7.03am

SSS MANOEUVRE
Known as such by military folk and not to be confused with SAS or SOS, this toilette trio involves cleaning self, top-to-toe, internally and externally. Enough said. No need to spell it out.

7.50am

MORNING MIRROR MANTRA
Smile at reflection, congratulate self on cleanliness and general appearance and say 'Today is a good day. I will win the pitch/game/contract /deal/bet...' (select motivational motto of your choice). Repeat.

9am

RELAX, IT'S SUNDAY
If it is the weekend, then all of these can be done at a much more leisurely pace. Have a DIY spa cleanse and chill, body and mind. Exfoliate, use a body brush, deep-cleanse and moisturize.

10am

FEET FIRST
Take the opportunity to control body hair and do foot care. Deal with cracked heels, Athlete's Foot, nail fungus, smelly feet, blisters...Perform a body MOT. Think of the bathroom as a garage.

however, you can spend more time on your hygiene routine, hours even. Dip in and out of the following regime as it fits your circumstances. Let it inspire you to do more. Let it freshen up your ideas. Let it wash over you.

7.05am

VA VA GROOM

Cleanse and shave (see pp 58–9). Nice warm shower (not too long, don't waste water), wash all parts thoroughly and end with a cold conclusion (just a few seconds) to liven up the system and close the pores.

7.30am

TO BE(ARD) OR NOT TO BE(ARD)

If you are going for growth and therefore not shaving, do trim facial furniture. Check orifices for unwanted guests. Shaving balm, anti-perspirant, moisturizer, touch of cologne...

7.45am

FLOSSER OR DOSSER

Floss teeth, brush them well (choose between manual or power-steering), swill of mouthwash and smile. Call on the FBI – floss, brush, irrigate – every day to keep dental bills at bay.

1pm

CHECK, CHECK, CHECK

Clean teeth at the office after lunch. Keep a brush and toothpaste in your desk. Check appearance in mirror. Quick brush of hair, maybe a quick go with a deo wipe (great invention).

6-7pm

AT THE END OF THE DAY

Freshen up when you get back from work or prepare to go out straight from the office. Repeat lunchtime routine. Splash of cologne (go easy, guys). Check no spinach on your teeth. Best foot forward. Check those too...

10pm

H2O BEFORE YOU GO

Clean teeth, cleanse face and moisturize. Have a quick, warm shower before bed to make you clean and sleepy or a nice long bath, depending on time and water constraints.

Don't be a Bathroom Bozo

'House-proud Wise Guy WLTM similar with GSOH for long-term domestic bliss.'
No, it does not stand for 'good sense of humour.' GSOH means Great Safety,
Order and Hygiene. These attributes are key to a bathroom and a successful

 ## Domestic God's No-Nos

1. Up is a Downer

Leaving the toilet seat up is a habit that most of the male population indulge in. It may be a cliché, but it's so true, so make sure it's a definite no-no in the smallest room in the house. However practical it may be (no explanations required) it is not uplifting for others. It gives out too much information on what is after all a very personal activity in a highly private space. An intimate act should remain just that, with no circumstantial evidence. Respect the seating arrangements in the bathroom just as you do in the dining room.

2. Benchmark, Not Tidemark

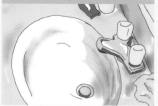

Devise and adhere to a bathroom routine that takes less than five minutes to complete yet saves you hours of anguish and work. One excellent preventative measure is to use bath or shower gel every time you run a bath – this reduces the likelihood or intensity of the tidemark and you'll come out of it smelling sweet. Clean the bath and the basin as soon as you can after use – the later you leave it, the longer it takes. Do it now, save a row. A bit of cream cleanser on a cloth, a touch of elbow grease.

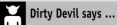

Dirty Devil says ...

Don't have a 'No Entry without a gas mask' sign on your bathroom door.

domestic partnership. To achieve and then keep them in place is your mission. Should you choose to accept it, you will need to get some no-no's under your belt. Here they are:

3. Roll On Roll Of *'in extremis'*

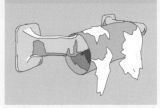

Ancient man may have made do with leaves and grass, modern man in extremis may resort to substitutes, but for the most part we prefer the stationery in the bathroom to be nice, soft toilet paper. Like waves in the ocean, when one roll has gone, another follows in its wake, not far behind. It's up to you to keep up this natural momentum. Replace one roll with another without leaving a hiatus. You don't want to embarrass guests or new friends, do you? Keep plentiful supplies of the stuff, with a replacement roll always on hand. Use an attractive basket to store them.

4. Old News is Bad News

You may like to catch up on the latest news in the smallest room but don't leave papers, magazines and nasty joke books strewn over the floor and surfaces, creating unnecessary clutter in a room intended for the three Rs. This is where you refresh, relax and restore. Take old news with you and recycle it. A bathroom can get hot and steamy and the last thing you need is damp, smelly, yellowing paper, curling at the edges as if embarrassed to be there. It isn't a library, after all. If you must treat it as a reading room, keep your literature (if it can be called that) in a neat pile or in a basket.

Bathroom Beauty

OK, now you have got what not to do under your belt, it is time for a touch of hygiene homework. Here's what you have to remember to do, regularly and repeatedly. It should become second nature to you. You know you thought the

Domestic God's Do-Dos

1. Get the Loo Down

About the worst job to have in the house is that of cleaning the toilet. Help it complete its tasks properly. Clean this overworked, life-changing invention daily if possible, more than once a week if not, disinfecting thoroughly and not forgetting under the rim. There lurk many mini monsters. Before flushing, put the lid down to avoid germs being ejected onto nearby surfaces. Cross-contamination is a big risk in bathrooms. Wipe the seat, clean the flush handle, then wash your hands in warm, soapy water.

2. Ventilate or Contaminate

Good ventilation is a vital part of keeping a home healthy, and it is particularly important in the bathroom. Condensation is an issue in any room where water is involved, and the bathroom will inevitably become humid after you have indulged in a hot shower or bath. Keep the window open or install an extractor fan to facilitate the exchange of dirty with clean air, wet with dry. Pesky house dust mites hate it when the air is dry. Try to keep the bathroom door closed in order to contain your steaminess.

Get fresh when things hot up. Open the window. Ventilate and anticipate.

fairies did the housework? Well, the bad news is, they don't exist. Does the truth hurt? Get over it. You always had your suspicions. It's DIY time. Focus, learn and digest. You will be tested on it later.

3. Desserts Not Deserts

Try to save water whenever you can. Bills look much more attractive and you are helping the environment. Some countries are really short of water and you can do your bit without sacrificing too much on the cleanliness stakes. When choosing a new toilet, get one with a quick and normal flush alternative (enough information already!). Time your showers, share baths (not with your dog), keep cold water from the shower in a bucket to use on the garden, don't leave the tap running when brushing your teeth and fix dripping taps.

4. Share Chores, Not Sores

Don't share towels – not with your beloved, pet, house mate, visiting parent or best friend. Washing towels can be a shared chore but nothing more. Communal bath towels harbour bacteria and viruses and can cross-contaminate. Damp towels are the worst. Dry your face and bath towels thoroughly between uses – outside or on a hot towel rail. Don't leave them on the bathroom floor (or the bed). Make sure each person has his or her own towel and knows which one it is. Colour code them if they are not too bright (the people not the towels).

Bathroom Confidential

Do you want to impress in the bathroom? Now's your chance to find out how. You have the world at your fingertips with the range of accessories available today. However, you should take care – some items are more ostentatious than

Use Or Pose: A Guide To The Stars

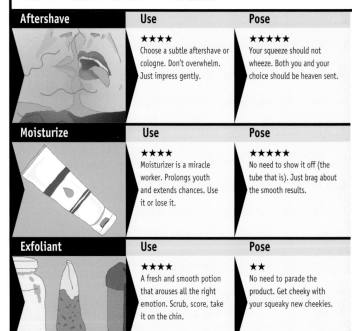

Aftershave	**Use**	**Pose**
	★★★★	★★★★★
	Choose a subtle aftershave or cologne. Don't overwhelm. Just impress gently.	Your squeeze should not wheeze. Both you and your choice should be heaven sent.
Moisturize	**Use**	**Pose**
	★★★★	★★★★★
	Moisturizer is a miracle worker. Prolongs youth and extends chances. Use it or lose it.	No need to show it off (the tube that is). Just brag about the smooth results.
Exfoliant	**Use**	**Pose**
	★★★★	★★
	A fresh and smooth potion that arouses all the right emotion. Scrub, score, take it on the chin.	No need to parade the product. Get cheeky with your squeaky new cheekies.

efficacious. You don't want to look like a bathroom buffoon. Use this chart when purchasing key items. It's a sort of bathroom confidential, so keep it on a 'need to know' basis only. Don't let anyone in on your new clean act.

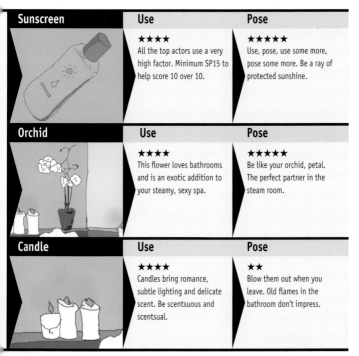

Sunscreen	Use	Pose
	★★★★ All the top actors use a very high factor. Minimum SP15 to help score 10 over 10.	★★★★★ Use, pose, use some more, pose some more. Be a ray of protected sunshine.
Orchid	Use	Pose
	★★★★ This flower loves bathrooms and is an exotic addition to your steamy, sexy spa.	★★★★★ Be like your orchid, petal. The perfect partner in the steam room.
Candle	Use	Pose
	★★★★ Candles bring romance, subtle lighting and delicate scent. Be scentsuous and scentsual.	★★ Blow them out when you leave. Old flames in the bathroom don't impress.

Tools: First Aid

It's important to have a first-aid kit on hand. Don't invest in a mini pharmacy, just a selection of key items with which to deal with minor accidents and common illnesses. Keep your supplies safe, well away from children and pets.

Lotions and Potions

Tea Tree Oil

This is a magic Australian potion, mate, and it's a no worries essential oil. It boasts anti-viral, antiseptic, antibiotic and anti-fungal properties. Bung some in the loo to disinfect it. Zap zits, burns and insect bites with it neat in very small amounts, too.

Bandages

Have a couple of cotton and crêpe bandages of different sizes in stock together with a large triangular one for a sling. Use for minor sprains, for holding dressings in place, excluding air from burns and immobilizing arms. Replace if you use to dress as a mummy.

Antiseptic Wipes

Keep alcohol free antiseptic wipes in stock for cuts and grazes (adults, not children). Remember it will sting but there's no gain without pain. Always wash the wound to remove dirt and grit etc. Don't reuse. Buy some more. Meanie. Get some antiseptic cream, too.

Have a list of important emergency numbers on hand and make sure everyone in the household knows where it is. Update it regularly. Key numbers into your phone. Keep details handy at all times.

First Aid Guidebook

It is very important to know your first aid. Keep the book on hand, make sure everyone in the house knows where it is and go on a first aid course – it's informative and even fun. You might meet a nice nurse and never need the book again.

Safety Pins

Large and small, even those big ones that people use for non-disposable nappies – keep them in stock. Keep them dry or they will go rusty. Don't use them to keep your trouser hem in place. This store is for the first aid to humans only. Buy your own for first aid to clothes.

Burn Ointment

If you suffer a minor burn, put it under cold running water for a couple of minutes. Do not apply butter. That is an old wives' tale and makes things much worse. The cold water removes the heat from the burn. Apply burn ointment and gauze to keep the air out.

Technique Tool Wisdom Cleaning Chore

Tools: Medicine Cabinet

Keep a well-stocked medicine cabinet and ensure it is childproof and away from prying eyes and jaws. Make sure the contents are well within their expiry dates and that anything unidentifiable is evicted. Review the contents, read

Important Equipment

Thermometer

Dump your mercury thermometer (safely) and use a digital one or a strip thermometer. This contains sensitive liquid crystal which changes colour with the reading. Use your thermometer to determine the presence or absence of fever and illness. Read instructions carefully.

Anti-Diarrhoea

You never know when you might need this. The product names differ but their effects are generally the same. Big meeting + bad tummy = big problem. Want-a-loo often follows vindaloo. Reach for the medication and head to the presentation. If symptoms persist, as they say, consult your doctor.

Plasters

Keep a selection of waterproof plasters or bandaids in the first aid box. Use for cuts and grazes and imaginary wounds (if nieces or nephews come to stay). Buy some of those plasters with cool designs if you are about to go to a big presentation or a hot date.

the labels, remove old stock and refresh supplies. This is a remedy resource not one that is ready to re-contaminate. Learn the difference between good and bad. It will help you in life.

Headache Tablets

Say goodbye to that dull ache with a mild painkiller. Too much to drink last night? Was the gig too loud and too late? Try to have tablets or liquid on hand (paracetamol, aspirin etc). Always take tablets with liquid – ie water (no, not more wine or beer). Always read instructions about dosage.

Scissors

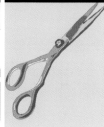

Keep a pair of sharp scissors in your medicine cabinet or first aid kit. If you rely on the kitchen scissors they will either be missing without leave or dirty. Use to cut bandages or plasters. Don't let anyone borrow them for sewing or hair-cutting.

Lavender Oil

Lavender oil is another essential oil and a must-have in the medicine cabinet. It can be used neat (again in small quantities) to heal burns and is used by aromatherapists to help colds, flu, stress, acne and sunburn, among other things. It relaxes and calms and is great in massage blends.

| Technique | Tool | Wisdom | Cleaning | Chore |

Tools: Self-Cleaning

Keep it clean, guys. You've heard that somewhere before. In the office or at the bar, perhaps? In the bathroom you need to keep everything really clean, squeakily so. And that means all the equipment – yours and that of the

DIY Beauty

Toothbrush

There is more to a toothbrush than meets the eye or mouth. Buy new, efficient ones regularly and only use those freebies from the airplane or hotel for single use. They are the equivalent of one-night stands in the bathroom. Not made for long-term relationships.

Dental Floss

It's the FBI. Floss, brush, irrigate. Flossing is not cool but its effects are. Deals with debris, attacks plaque and brightens breath. Do it every day – twice if you like. Then brush and swirl. Don't floss in meetings or during a nice dinner with a putative partner.

Tweezers

A man without tweezers is a man with ticks, splinters, superfluous facial furniture and bushy eyebrows. Invest in an expensive pair for greater accuracy and longer life. Buy two pairs in case your partner makes off with the first set.

equipment in the front line in the bathroom. There are lots of things on the market to help you. Choose wisely and you'll shine. Be a hygiene hero. Polish that halo. Smile with a zing of confidence.

Toothpaste	Spare Razor	Spare Toothbrush

You can never have enough toothpaste and there is no need to argue about how the tube is squeezed now that pump-action models are in town. You still need to put the lid back on. Lid down on the loo, lid back on toothpaste. How easy is that?	A spare razor is a good idea for guests (expected or surprise – lucky you!), crises (where did you leave yours?), bluntness (its rather than yours) and thieves (isn't that just like so annoying?). It shows concern, kindness, forethought and cunning.	Go one step further and invest in a few spare toothbrushes. Colour code if necessary (in your dreams). Buy nice sturdy ones – don't just keep the ones you used on that long haul flight. Don't be dentally retarded.

| Technique | Tool | Wisdom | Cleaning | Chore |

Good Bathroom/Bad Bathroom

OK, guys, deep breath. Open your bathroom door. What do you see? Actually, what you smell might be more appropriate. Are your eyes met with a clean, serene sanctuary scene and your nostrils filled with the delicate fragrance of a hygienic, non-toxic collection of body-cleansing instruments? If you were locked in your bathroom for a few days by accident (or the design of others)

 ## Bad Bathroom

A bad bathroom is full of evil intent. Intent to cross-contaminate, spread germs willy-nilly, provide the perfect conditions for noxious, toxic, nausea-inducing experiments and undermine your new status as Domestic God. It's worth remembering that guests coming for lunch, dinner or a night with a DVD and a Domestic God are more likely to visit this room unaccompanied than any other in your house and spend longer in there looking at your personal possessions and habits. Bear that in mind when you chuck clothes and damp towels on the floor, leave tidemarks in the bath and basin, stuff laundry in a box until it explodes, leave toothpaste on the tiles and other unsavoury reminders of your activities. The Dirty Devil just loves a Bad Bathroom. So many ways to be unpleasant. Stop him in his tracks.

Clean and clear, healthy and hygienic, germ-free... you and your bathroom.

Approach with care, don't touch, wear marigolds...

would you perish due to the concentration of germs? Would you become another bacterial experiment yourself? This room must be champion of the hygiene league. Don't get relegated. You won't pull the crowds if you do.

✔ Good Bathroom

A good bathroom has a lovely clean mirror in it for a very good reason – to reflect your healthy hygiene habits and your rather smug but sparkling grin. A good bathroom is free of clutter, its dust-free shelves and surfaces sport only essential items, its floor is barren of dirty clothes and foul-smelling towels. Its toilet is clean enough to eat lunch from, its plugholes clear and fresh-scented, its bath inviting and its shower curtain mould-free. Guests will feel confident of emerging from the room cleaner than when they entered. They do not sport boots, marigolds and goggles before daring to enter. A bathroom should be a place in which to rest and recuperate. Its goal is not to provoke panic and pollution. Got the message now?

The Roman Latrine

Next time you are in your bathroom alone, enjoying a moment of peace and privacy in your most intimate acts of hygiene, travel back in time mentally to Roman days when things were rather more communal. Romans were considerably less shy about bodily functions than we tend to be today. They would perform their ablutions in public without turning a hair (as it were).

Roman latrines were constructed in a long line, sometimes equipped with marble seats. It was rather like sitting on a tube train on your way to work but with a different kind of motion involved.

Historians are not sure if both sexes performed their daily rituals at the same time and in the same place, but it is possible. Roman togas had all angles covered, but they could not disguise other side effects.

Romans were well aware of the need for hygiene. Their loo roll took the form of sponges on sticks and they would wash their hands at a basin before leaving. Sewers under the baths would wash their waste to the river and the water flowed continuously, making the Roman latrine the first 'flushing loo.' There were very few loos at home in those days, so public lavatories really were just that.

The whole bathing business was a very important part of Roman life. It played a key role in the daily regime of men of all classes and for many women. The *thermae* (baths) were an early version of the health spas and clubs of today, but they didn't cost an arm and a leg. The complex would include a library, lecture hall and promenade, making it a cultural and intellectual centre.

Compare and contrast your own hygiene routine with that of an average Roman guy. Up at sunrise to start work, back home about noon and then off to the communal baths from 2pm. Lots of ablutions with potions and lotions by slaves, a spot of sport, the odd interesting lecture, leisurely chats about the market and who's invading where and then home for a good dinner. He would move from the warm room or *tepidarium* to the hot bath or *caldarium* and then back to the *tepidarium* before a spell in the cold room or *frigidarium* and a final, refreshing dip in the cold pool. Puts your quick shower to shame, but you could learn a lesson or two by rising early to spend more time on your 'toilette' (your regime, not your loo, guys) in a leisurely and thorough fashion. You too could emerge refreshed, scrubbed, relaxed and ready for the day.

Bathing Creatively

Getting clean can be fun and relaxing. Enjoy the experience and experiment with ways of increasing the pleasure factor. Here are some cheap and cheerful ways. No need to splash out to splash out.

Head Massage

Sit up in the bath, relax your neck and close your eyes. Imagine your head is suspended from above. Breathe in deeply and exhale slowly, emptying your lungs. Count ten deep breaths in this way, keeping your head and neck relaxed. Open your eyes, think about something nice, and smile. Life feels good.

Do Real Men Exfoliate?

Even a rhinoceros exfoliates, so if it's good enough for such a majestic animal to wallow in mud, it's good enough for you. For as long as time itself, sand, ash and salt have been used by humans as an important pampering medium. Strawberries, pineapples and bananas make excellent natural exfoliators and rubbing avocado peel on your face is a good way of removing dead skin cells. If this all sounds a bit fruity, use a commercial face scrub. Your face will feel as smooth as a baby's bottom.

Do it Like Cleopatra

For a truly Roman experience, pour some fresh organic milk in to the bath –

pretend it is full of breakfast cereal and use enough for about three bowlfuls. Antony certainly seemed to like it. If you're in the mood for more of a cocktail soak, add coconut milk, yoghurt and honey (around a tablespoon of each) and a mashed banana. Relax – you'll eat your words.

Stubble Trouble

If things cut up rough on the chin front try an oil that has aloe vera, peppermint, tea tree oil or vitamin E in it. Find one that has all four and you'll smile from ear to ear.

Veg Out

Placing a slice of cucumber on each eye is both relaxing and refreshing. Hey, who's looking at you? If someone comes in to the room, eat them. Lemon juice can be used to soften the skin and cleanse stained hands. Tomatoes moisturize and act as good toners, while aloe vera soothes and nourishes your skin. Buy an aloe vera plant, cut off a stem then squeeze the juice directly onto the skin.

Put Your Foot in It

While a long, bare-footed stroll on a sandy beach is the best way to exfoliate your feet, peppermint lotion is excellent for freshening up odorous extremities. And in the absence of the ocean, some mashed banana with a teaspoon of honey and a dash of lime juice is a good homemade alternative. If you're feeling fruity, spread it all over your feet, don a pair of cotton socks and keep them on overnight. You will awake feeling top banana.

Relax Standing Up

If you like a bit of suffering, rub your body with dead sea salt as you shower (ordinary sea salt will do if you run out). Leave on for a few minutes, rinse off and dry yourself with fluffy warm towels. It feels like a long swim in the ocean. Moisturize all over and do some gentle exercise.

Take Care with Hair

Don't use shower or bath gel to wash your hair. Stick to shampoo. Shower gel often contains powerful detergents and usually a good dose of fragrance, both of which could damage your hair. Interestingly, beer is good for hair (externally applied, of course).

Toilet Tactics: Flushed with Success

Toilets are made of strong stuff – they have to be. Theirs is one of the toughest jobs in the house. They are front line operatives and deserve respect. Neglect them at your peril. Germs, odours and other unwanted side effects will

Unblocking a Toilet – Sorting a Sluggish Flush

1

Toilets get blocked – it happens. Take a large, long-handled open-flange plunger (hire one if necessary) and place over the drain opening at the base of the bowl, having bailed out excess water. Leave enough to cover the plunger cup. Pump up and down with vigour (about ten times), finishing with a final flourish (if not flush).

2

To find out if the flush holes in the rim are fully open, hold a mirror under the toilet bowl rim at an angle that allows you to see the holes. If you borrow your partner's mirror, make sure you wash it thoroughly afterwards or it will reflect badly on you.

3

To unblock the rim flush holes, cut a short section of wire from a coat hanger and insert carefully in each hole, taking care not to damage the porcelain. Turn the wire to loosen mineral deposits that may have built up there.

4

If this tactic fails, you may want to hire a WC auger – a flexible rod with a crank handle at one end. The flexible part goes into the trap and you need to crank the handle with care (usually clockwise, but check instructions) to dislodge the pesky blockage.

follow. If you have noticed that friends never use your bathroom, ask yourself why. It may be a No-Go area for reasons of hygiene rather then privacy. Think safety, cleanliness and appeal. Toilets need them all.

Toilette Techniques

FLOOR STYLE
Always pick up your wet towel and hang it up to dry. Wash your towel regularly, and well before it develops an unpleasant, stale odour. Put bathroom mats in the wash every week, too.

TOP TOILET TIP
Borrow (permanently) a couple of denture-cleaning tablets from your grandparents and pop them into the toilet. Leave them overnight to do their thing and then brush and flush. Smile.

ODOUR EATER
Light a match to banish unwanted odours. This really works. Blow out match and place in bin. Whilst on the subject, don't smoke in the bathroom. Ever.

THE DRAIN GAME
To combat smelly drains without using bleach, try flushing boiling water and a handful of salt down the drain. Congealed grease will be dissolved.

HAIR TODAY
Wash your combs and brushes regularly – twice a month if possible. They may look fine, but natural oils from your hair and shampoo residues build up on your hair care products as well as on your scalp. Wash in warm water and mild detergent and rinse well (your comb, not your scalp).

HOME AND AWAY HYGIENE
An old, dirty travelling wash bag is a no-no. When visiting friends, don't empty its nasty contents all over their clean bathroom surfaces, particularly if you have a soap container that looks more like a petrie dish and a toothbrush that looks as if it has seen some serious action. Buy a travel set of toiletries and tools and keep them clean and contemporary.

CLEAN TOILET, GIVE ME FIVE
5 minutes spent, 50 calories burned, 5 million germs zapped.

Cleaning the Bath and Shower

Bathing was an important activity for the Romans and they sure had the right idea about it. Their public baths were multi-media entertainment centres for clean folk boasting libraries, gardens, walkways, balconies for sunbathing, theatres for poetry readings and music as well as a wide range of cleansing opportunities. For many of us today, relaxing in the bath continues to be one of life's great pleasures. It's as near as we get to a trip back into the womb.

If, however, at the end of a hard day we are greeted by a dirty tub with an obvious and nasty ring around it, the pleasure of bathtime is somewhat diminished. Don't just close your eyes and climb in. Give it a good clean using a cloth and an appropriate non-abrasive cleaner – dishwashing liquid will dissolve stubborn residue. If you run out of commercial products or simply prefer to make your own, use a paste of bicarbonate of soda and water on a damp cloth and apply with elbow grease. Listen to the radio as you do this or practise your speech for the following day at the office. Your voice will sound encouragingly impressive. Rinse the bath thoroughly. Always use different cloths and sponges for the bath, toilet and walls or you will cross-contaminate. Keep them clean by giving them a regular wash in the machine, using hot water or by soaking in a solution of bleach and water. Grey, crusty cloths that lurk on the floor must be banished from the bathroom.

Naked Housework

Why not try a spot of nude housework? Not as kinky as it sounds, it's quite a practical way of keeping your shower clean. Climb in and do the job in your birthday suit. Give the tiles and glass screens a wipe down using a sponge and a commercial tile and glass cleaner or use convenient bathroom wipes. You could try a spot of DIY by using a spray bottle filled with white vinegar. This will help keep limescale at bay. Spray on the surface, leave for a few minutes, rinse off and buff (in the buff). For all these substances, avoid contact with the skin. Emerge from the shower in reverse as you tackle the floor with a more robust, non-abrasive creamy cleaner. Rinse well. You could now climb back in and give yourself a wash down. Sing as you clean to release those all-important feel-good hormones.

If you have a plastic shower curtain, keep it clean or it will go mouldy. Sponge it with water and bicarbonate of soda or

Leave the bathroom as you yourself
would like to find it – clean and
welcoming. This should not be a
Hard Hats Only zone. It's a private,
personal space.

The smallest room equals smallest
amount of housework, surely. It
doesn't add up otherwise. Wrong
again... Womb doesn't begin and
end with 'b'.

put in the washing machine with some
old, colourfast towels. Put on a warm
wash but don't spin. Hang the curtain
immediately. Chrome taps and

showerheads can be washed with non-
abrasive bathroom cleaners or a soft cloth
dipped in white vinegar. Dry and buff (not
in the buff this time, necessarily).

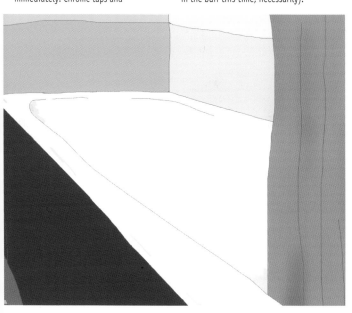

Cleaning the Sink and Mirror

Bathroom hygiene is of paramount importance but needn't be too taxing on muscles or patience. Those of you who live alone may think you don't need to do much in the bathroom. Wrong. Keep the air circulating – open the windows as often and as wide as you can – and keep the room warm and dry.

Mirror

Use a clean cloth dipped in a solution of water with just a hint of vinegar and then polish with a newspaper to achieve an old-fashioned gleam.

If you prefer the more modern approach, use a glass cleaner spray but spray the cloth rather than the mirror and work from the middle outwards. That way the liquid won't run around the edges, causing the silver to oxidize and turn black. Once polished to perfection, admire your reflection.

Basins

Clean your porcelain basin with a creamy non-abrasive cleaner (or bathroom wipes). Once a surface is cracked, germs move in. Rinse the clean

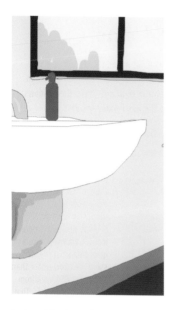

Bidet

More and more bathrooms boast bidets nowadays. Once you have worked out how to use your particular model, make sure you keep it clean. Treat your bidet as you would your bath or sink. Wash its exterior, but remember to disinfect the interior. Use an old toothbrush to clean inside the overflow. Don't use it for anything else!

Out with the Grout

A cleaner containing bleach will help tackle unattractive discoloration in your grouting. Use an old nailbrush or toothbrush to clean it but don't splash the cleaner on the carpet, curtains or yourself. You might find it easier to replace the grouting if it is really nasty or to buy some special grout paint in one of many colours.

basin and dry thoroughly. It will look shiny and lovely – perfect for your guest. Stainless steel stinks can be washed with a dishwashing detergent. Rinse and dry. Avoid harsh abrasive cleansers.

Cabinets

Give them a spring clean from time to time. Decant contents, clean shelves and only put back those items you use regularly and medicine that is current and identifiable. Dispose of medication safely.

Cleaning Floors

Keep the floor clean and dry in the bathroom. It's as simple as that. This is a wet room, in the true meaning of the term. Wet people, wet hair, wet feet (even the odd wet pet or two), wet clothes, lots of liquids in plastic bottles – lots of lids left off them. It is a spill-fest waiting to happen. Keep it clean and dry, ventilated and aired. Don't be floored, don't be flawed.

Carpets

If you have a carpet in your bathroom, make sure you use (and clean, regularly) a bathmat. If you get the carpet damp by dripping on it as you emerge from the bath or shower, it will get musty and damaged. It will stain and perish. Why not get a nice rug if it is a large room – much easier to clean than a carpet, particularly if it is machine washable. Don't let your pet leave numero uno messages on it, please. Return to sender asap if they do – well, not literally. That would be too cruel. Use the BBS technique (blot, blot, solution). If your dog brings mud in (or indeed if your guest or housemate does, leave it to dry first and then vacuum it up (the mud, not the housemate).

Other Flooring

You may have one of many flooring options in the bathroom. Some people have wood, others tiles, linoleum, vinyl or cork. If you are about to choose a floor, why not consider underfloor heating and really pamper your feet if not your budget. Mmm, lovely warm floor on a chilly morning. What could be nicer and tempt you into the shower when it is freezing outside? Whichever surface you have, keep it clean, keep it dry. Employ the DVS team (dusting, sweeping and vacuuming, that well known trio) to sort the pitch out first and then send on your cleaning players. Once they have

Solid Hardwood Floors

LIQUID SPILLS (water, coffee, wine, etc.) left for any length of time on the floor will cause stains. Wipe up spills as soon as they happen.

LADIES with high heels and dangerous stilettos can leave an impression on you and your floor. Ask them politely to remove their perilous footwear – everyone will feel more comfortable.

PETS with long nails and weak bladders scratch and stain wood. Train your pets and trim their claws (sadly, felt pads don't work on dogs and cats).

SHOES with damaged heels equal potential damage. Repair your shoes regularly and check your partner and housemates do the same. Guests are harder to boss around.

sorted the opposition, bring on the detergent striker and score. MRD (mop and rinse and dry) are your guys for the job.

Linoleum

Linoleum is an increasingly popular choice for flooring. Based on linseed oil and finely ground cork, it is natural and environmentally sound and you will be delighted to discover that not only is it nice underfoot but it also has the power to destroy bacteria on the floor naturally. Less work for you, better result. Sweep or vacuum gently and then mop with warm water and detergent. Dry thoroughly. You can remove marks with steel wool dipped in turpentine. Scrub gently.

Vinyl

Again sweep or vacuum gently and mop with nice detergenty water. If you fancy polishing it, use a water-based emulsion polish.

Cork Floors

If you have a cork floor, take extra care. Vacuum or sweep regularly but resist the temptation to rush off and get the mop and bucket. Remember, cork floors are made from the cork tree and are therefore organic. They need to be cleaned with appropriate specialist liquids and waxes. Ask your local hardware store to advise you. Always deal with spills as soon as they occur. You may well prevent the formation of stains by so doing. Act now, no need to repent later.

Don't allow cork to get too wet. Dry it thoroughly after washing.

Use a bathmat. Please. Puddles are so out. Nice, sparkling and dry floors are so in. Keep on top of floor fashion, don't tip your toe onto flawed floors please guys.

| Technique | Tool | Wisdom | Cleaning | Chore |

Stain Removal

Stains are inevitable within the home, however much care you may take to prevent them, but the quicker you act, the more successful you are likely to be at removing them. Deal, don't disguise. Heal, don't hide.

Stain Removal Kit (SRK)

Every household needs a Stain Removal Kit (SRK) primed for action at any moment. For general household incidents, the following equipment is all you need. Photocopy the list and take it to the store:

- ABSORBENT PAPER TOWELS OR SPONGES
- CLEAN, ABSORBENT WHITE CLOTHS
- ALL-PURPOSE DETERGENT
- WHITE VINEGAR
- WHITE SPIRIT
- BLEACH
- AMMONIA
- NON-OILY NAIL VARNISH REMOVER
- LAUNDRY STAIN PRE-TREATMENT PRODUCT
- SPECIALIST STAIN REMOVERS (FOR THINGS LIKE BALLPOINT OR FELT-TIP STAINS)
- RUBBING ALCOHOL
- BICARBONATE OF SODA
- SOLVENT-TYPE CLEANING FLUIDS OR DRY-CLEANING FLUIDS
- NON-SOLVENT STAIN OR SPOT REMOVER
- LEMONS

FLOORS

Before you set about removing stains from wood flooring, it is important to ascertain if the stain or scratch is in the wood itself or on the topcoat finish.

NATURAL- OR WAX-FINISH FLOORS / FLOORS WITHOUT HARD FINISHES Gently rub the stain with a damp cloth, rub dry and then wax. Again, the working-from-outside-in principle applies. Water stains should be rubbed with steel wool and then waxed. White rings can be removed using a paste of salt and olive oil left on the stain overnight. Wipe off the next morning and re-wax.

WOOD FLOORS WITH HARD FINISHES OR VARNISHES, INCLUDING POLYURETHANE Care needs to be taken with such floors (you can detect them by checking to see if the stain is in the superficial finish). Scratches should be repaired with specialist kits available from flooring retailers and other stains should be treated with specialist cleaners for urethane finishes.

Removing a Stain

1	2	3	4
Don't waste time. Grab some paper towel and act. Pulling a rug over the stain won't help. Ignoring it won't make it go away. It's like toothache. Think SBS – scoop, blot, solution. If it's a liquid spill, it's more of a BBS – blot, blot solution technique. Blot with paper towel or a soft, clean and colourfast cloth.	If the spill is solid or semi-solid, you need to scoop up as much of it as you can with a spoon, spatula or similar blunt object. Don't use a carving knife – cutting out a stain is not a solution. Be careful to contain the spill. Don't play with it or rub it into the carpet. This is serious stuff and you need to get a grip.	Now is the time to apply the cleaning substance. Use a mixture of detergent and water or a specialist stain remover. Read the instructions. It's a good idea to do a test patch first in an inconspicuous spot. Apply the cleaning substance directly to the stain, give it time to do its work and then blot clean.	The final tactic is to spray lukewarm water over the offending area and blot as usual. Once the carpet is dry, gently brush or vacuum the area to restore its pile and glory. You may need to repeat this process. If you fancy steam- or dry-cleaning your carpets, call in the professionals.

WALLS AND PAINTWORK

Unwanted scribbling on the walls calls for bicarbonate of soda diluted with a little water in a small bowl to form a thick paste. Rub gently on the offending mark.

Stain removal on wallpaper is a tricky business and you may end up making things worse. Choose from a wide selection of commercial substances, including solvents, but follow instructions carefully and check they are safe for your type of wallpaper. Sometimes, rubbing dirty patches with stale white bread has been known to work (who said household management was predictable).

Technique Tool Wisdom Cleaning Chore

Here's Lurking at You

Mould is one of the biggest problems in the bathroom. It is unsightly and looks daunting – a bit like your own reflection in the morning after a heavy night. Fear not, the Little Book of Wisdom can help. First of all, don't despair. Let in the fresh air. Keep the sparkle in the bathroom and your love life.

Mould – Out with the Old

1

Open all the windows. Put on some protective clothing. Try some brightly coloured rubber gloves (they will cheer you up).

2

Check out where the offending areas are – probably on the top of the walls and the ceiling. Eviction time has come. It is your job to clean up your bathroom act. OK, so it is not a particularly sexy job, but just think how the bathroom will become a top romantic spot instead of a health and hygiene hotspot.

3

Use a mixture of household bleach (1 part) and water (2 parts) and a cloth. You can mix the solution in a bucket of water, but keep rinsing the cloth out in fresh running water under the tap or you risk spreading the mould spores over other surfaces. Rinse off any excess bleach with clean water. Allow the surface to dry.

4

You can also use mildew-proof bathroom paint if you fancy trying a more permanent answer to the problem. It does not actually kill mildew but its special resin stops it growing back. A water-based paint that usually comes with a guarantee to remain mildew-proof for 5 years when applied correctly, it has a finish that isn't affected by moisture. Why not have a go?

Dirty Devil says ...

Let's get Mould and Mildew round and have a party. Wall to wall party, guys.

Domestic God says ...

Make Mould old news. Say 'Farewell, Mildew, it's over.'
Kiss goodbye to Musty.

5

Ventilation not hibernation is the order of the day. Being able to open the window is important – you need to ventilate the bathroom on a regular basis. It's important to get rid of steam as it causes condensation to form which will encourage mould to return. If the windows are stuck or there are no windows, install an effective steam extractor.

6

Clean the rest of the bathroom while you are at it. Hey, is the shower head clogged up? Remove the head, unblock the holes by poking them with a darning needle (borrow one from your granny or have a go with a cocktail stick) and then rinse the head with white vinegar.

7

Anything removable and portable, take out into the sunny garden to dry thoroughly. No, not your housemate.

8

Mould and mildew just love setting up home in shower curtains. The easiest way to keep them homeless is to buy two curtains that you can safely bung in the machine and alternate. Pop the dirty curtain in the machine with a couple of towels and hang it up to dry (outside if possible). You don't want to put a damp curtain back in the bathroom.

Soap

Historians assure us that soap was first made around the first century A.D. and archaeologists found what they thought to be the first soap factory in the ancient city of Pompeii. Soap, it seems, was first used for washing cloth rather than skin and was far from the gentle and pleasantly perfumed product it is today. Early versions of soap were made of fats and oils mixed with an alkaline solution. The mixture was boiled together in large vats, salt was added and when the process was complete, the soap would rise to the top of the vessel.

The Science of Soap

Each soap molecule is made up of carbon, hydrogen and oxygen atoms. It has a head composed of carboxyl, which is hydrophilic, ie loves water, and a hydrocarbon tail that is hydrophobic, ie afraid of water, but just adores oil and grease (does it sound like your housemate?).

1. Your skin looks like this before a shower or bath. Attractive? Not. Time to ablute.

2. Now you're in the shower and the soap is on your skin. It has made contact and is preparing for take-off.

3. The hydrophobic end of the soap molecules is desperate to escape. The hydrophilic end is fatally attracted to the water. It takes the grime with it as it goes.

4. Together they accomplish the mission. It's lift-off for dirt. Phew! (or rather, not phew).

Surface Tension

Next time you step into the shower, notice how water forms beads on the surface of your skin. This is because the surface tension of the water prevents it from reaching and clinging to the skin. When soap is introduced to your skin, the hydrophobic end of the soap molecule tries to get as far away from the water as possible, whereas the water-loving end is fatally attracted to the H2O. The result is a film that breaks the surface tension.

Fatal Attraction

Your body is covered with a protective layer of oil secreted by your skin. This forms a barrier that prevents dirt and particles from entering your pores, but (sadly for some) you look dirty because the dirt trapped in the layer is visible to the naked eye. When soap is applied, the oil and grease-loving tails of the molecules attach themselves to the oily layer. When water is added, the water-loving head of the soap molecule pulls the dirty tail off the skin, removing the grime and grease with it, leaving you clean. How simple is that?

Soap Opera

Today, soap is big business. Manufacturers slice it, sculpt it, square it up, scent, spice and shave it and even suspend things in it. It comes in all shapes and sizes.

Domestic God says ...

Putting Soap on the Ropes

Selecting the right soap for you is a very personal affair. Don't just grab the first bar on the shelf. Choosing soap is like finding the right partner. Popeye probably enjoys washing with Olive Oil. Others may not. Ask a professional to identify your skin type and recommend a suitable soap.

Skin – Scratch the Surface

It helps to understand the contents of soap, but first, let's examine its target surface – your outer layer of skin or epidermis. It is thickest on your feet and thinnest on your face. You can scrub your feet with soap and water energetically but you need to be much more careful with the skin on your face.

Keep it Clean, Guys

Remember that if you don't wash, you will encourage germs and dirt to gather, settle and multiply on your skin. It's like walking around covered in a filthy carpet. Not a good look. You will be covered in bugs, not hugs. Who wants to kiss a carpet covered in crumbs?

Pampering

You are about to enjoy some 'Domestic God Me Time'. You may feel inclined to lock the door – that's entirely your decision – but remember that a back massage from your partner might be a good way to end your spa.

Set the Scene

Turn off the lights and let the candles illuminate the scene as the bath fills with warm water. Select music and play (gently does it). Pour six to eight drops of essential oil (lavender, bergamot and camomile are particularly calming) into the water. Different oils have different effects so a little pre-purchase research is worth the effort. The steam and warmth evaporate the oils and give off a wonderful aroma while softening your skin. You will feel uplifted as well as relaxed, soothed as well as restored. Choose an essential oil with a scent that appeals, add a few drops into a pump spray and dilute with water to make your own air freshener. It's that easy. If you feel awkward shopping for such 'pampering' items, pretend the oils are for your mother, or opt for a more anonymous on-line shopping experience.

Gadgets

There are numerous gadgets around that increase the relaxation factor once you are immersed. An inflatable waterproof pillow, a machine that transforms the

bath into a whirling Jacuzzi, a foot spa and a battery-powered massager are just a few of the items that can create an out-of-this-world, out-of-water experience. None of these are as essential as the oils though – the warm water, the oils and the opportunity to debrief are highly effective in their own right.

Playing Footsie

Now that you're relaxed and refreshed, it is time to cut the toe nails (see page 128) and give yourself a foot scrub with a brush or pumice stone. Read a magazine or meditate. Think nice thoughts. Out with hate, in with love.

Conditioning

To condition the skin, mix pre-mashed avocado with a teaspoon of honey (you can do this in the bath) and apply liberally to your face as a mask, avoiding the eye area. Relax for 15 minutes and then rinse off with warm water. Nobody needs to know you've been dousing yourself with vegetation in the name of body maintenance. While you are at it, you could consider rubbing mashed banana on to your hair to condition it the natural way. Rinse well before using conventional shampoo.

Exercise

Indulge in some bath exercises to improve muscle tone, but remember not to get your toe stuck in the tap. Don't laugh – it does happen. Stretch your legs, massage them gently and tense buttock muscles.

Moisturize your body after a bath, while your skin is warm and absorbent.

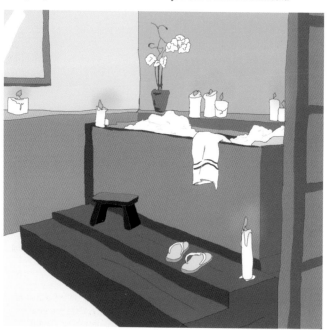

| Technique | Tool | Wisdom | Cleaning | Chore |

Wet Shaving

When you can't sleep try and calculate how many times in your life to date you have shaved? How many hours will you spend de-stubbling? How much shaving foam will you get through? How many razors will you buy? Zzzzzzzzzzzzz... (Still awake? Grow a beard).

Stubborn Stubble, Blade Runner to the Rescue

Do-Dos

- Shave in a warm room with lots of warm water
- Always use a good blade
- Warm it in the sink or under hot running water
- Always shave the face in the direction of the beard growth, rinsing the blade in hot water regularly
- In tricky areas (chin and under the nose) move the blade sideways across the growth not against it
- Rinse well with cool water and pat dry gently
- Moisturize after shaving
- Apply cologne (just a dash) behind your ears
- Rinse your brush and razor thoroughly to remove soap
- Flick to get rid of most of the water
- Hang your brush on a brush stand

No-Nos

- Don't shave 'against the grain' of the beard
- Even in tricky zones, don't shave against the growth – it will pull the skin in the wrong direction and call cuts and grazes, aka razor burn, razor rash or in-grown hairs
- Don't apply alcohol-based products to your face after shaving (ouch)
- Don't put your damp brush back in a closed cupboard or wash bag for any length of time or mildew may set in.
- Don't share razors with your partner, even if they ask really, really nicely
- Don't use blunt razors
- Don't buy the cheapest shaving equipment, buy the best you can afford

Enjoy a Really Close Shave

1 Yawn, Warm, Wet

After cleansing your face first thing in the morning, it's time to shave (unless you are going for that Desperate Dan Gets an Office Job look). A wet shave is kinder to the skin than an electric one. In an ideal world, you would use electric razors from time to time only. A wet shave has a peeling effect and helps care for your skin. If you have acne or other skin problems it can make them worse, however. Washing your face with warm water first softens the facial hair and makes a close shave easier. Try shaving after a bath or shower. Why not soak a flannel in hot water and wrapping it around your face for a minute. Too long? OK, 30 seconds.

2 Froth, Foam, Face Facts

Don't froth up with a normal bar of soap – it just does not have the properties needed for a comfortable, close shave. Invest in some good equipment – some nice shaving cream, soap, gel or mousse and a good quality brush (put a really nice badger brush on your Christmas list). You need to work up a real lather to help the razor glide smoothly over your skin without causing damage. If you are using shaving cream, place a small amount in the palm of one hand, dip the brush into hot water and work up a lather using a nice circular motion (bit like dusting but more micro and contained). Use a similar circular motion to apply the lather to your wet face and make the hairs stand proud, ready to be tackled and felled like rugby players at a final. Dip brush in warm water if you need more moisture. If you are using soap, use the same circular motion but apply it to the bar itself. Try leaving the cream, soap, foam, gel, mousse or shaving soap on your face for a couple of minutes before you go blading. They help prepare the skin and may extend the lifespan of your razor. Mousse is a good choice on the cost and consistency front. Research the products on the shelves before you decide which suits you.

DIY Remedies

You don't need to go all herbal burble, guys, but it's worth learning more about a few homemade remedies for minor complaints. Read on to find out about

Home Remedies

SORE THROAT Gargle with warm salt water and then drink a 50/50 mixture of fresh lemon juice and honey. Add boiling water to the lemon and honey to make a soothing hot drink.

CUTS, BURNS AND INSECT BITES Undiluted lavender oil can be applied directly on to burns and cuts to help them heal quickly.

EARACHE Apply a little warm olive oil into the ear to relieve the pain. Keep your head at a slant when applying the oil, to avoid it slipping out over your face – you are not a salad.

GINGER It's great in early morning fruit smoothies. It brings zing to the day. Put a few drops of ginger

oil in hot water to make a fab foot bath and combat colds and flu. Careful if you have sensitive skin.

ECHINACEA Echinacea is an immune enhancer, a natural antibiotic, antiseptic and tonic. You can buy it as tablets, tea or a tincture. It is thought to be good at warding off colds and flu. Ask in your local health store about dosage. Keep some in your cabinet.

TEA TREE OIL Tea tree oil has antiseptic, antibiotic, anti-viral and anti-fungal properties. Use it for zits, burns and insect bites. A few drops in the bath will cleanse and purify your body. Always keep an eye on the use-by date of oils.

PEPPERMINT OIL This is one of the oldest household remedies, traditionally used for upset tummies, indigestion, fever and colic. It is used in aftershaves and skin tonics because of its invigorating properties. Peppermint tea aids digestion and peppermint oil capsules are available to help colic, nausea and indigestion. The oil can be applied to the temples to stop headaches.

GARLIC Garlic is cultivated for both culinary and medicinal purposes. It has natural antibiotic properties and helps fight coughs and colds. If the raw stuff is not to your taste, buy yourself some odourless garlic capsules.

lotions, potions and sorting your emotions. It's like a walk-in feel-better larder. You will have to stock up on items – the shopping fairies are all on strike.

ALOE VERA Grow this as a houseplant and use its juice to moisturize, treat cold sores, abrasions and burns.

HONEY Hippocrates realized the power of honey way back in the 1st century BC. It has been used as a healing agent for wounds, burns and cuts over the centuries. Try a teaspoon of honey in a cup of warm milk with a drop of vanilla extract and it may help on the zzzzzzzz front on sleepless nights. Some people swear by applying honey at night to their toes and the nasty bits in between to sort Athlete's foot. Wear socks in bed with your partner or you may incur other injuries!

POSITIVE THINKING If you are feeling rather stressed, why not try a spot of positive thinking in the shower. No you can't go out and buy it at the pharmacist. It's not hope on a rope. You have to relax and fill your mind with positive, optimistic messages. Think of a sentence in the present tense with just one concept and no negatives and repeat. 'I am good at my job' would be a good example. 'I am good at housework' will help motivate you when all the dusting, vacuuming and polishing gets too much.

Technique	Tool	**Wisdom**	Cleaning	Chore

Hangovers from Hell

Your head is throbbing, the bathroom is spinning, your tummy is decidedly queasy – has someone smuggled you onto a pirate ship? No, you have a hangover and that's why you look so awful in the mirror. You are most likely to feel the pain and see the horror of your over-indulgence in the bathroom, so make it a centre of excellence in control and remedy. Learn why you get a hangover, how you can recover and how to avoid another one like it.

Why does it Hurt so Much?

- You are dehydrated. Alcohol is a diuretic and removes fluids from the body – hence that awful thirst, sandpaper mouth, headache and dizziness. The alcohol has irritated your stomach and it's in a bad mood. Your partner is in a bad mood. Everybody is in a bad mood.

- You have probably only slept for a few hours. You feel tired. Your body is tired, having spent all night trying to recover from the punishment you have put it through. Everybody is tired.

- You are embarrassed about what happened, your body is embarrassed, your friends are embarrassed. Everybody is embarrassed. Everything hurts.

What Can I Do About It?

- You could take a paracetamol for your headache. Aspirin may upset your stomach. So keep you bathroom cabinet stocked with both of these remarkable remedies.

- Replace lost vitamins and minerals and flush out those toxins while rehydrating. Drink water and fruit juice. Vitamin C tablets are a good idea.

- Try eating some toast and if that stays down, have some eggs – they are full of cysteine, a compound that is thought to mop up the destructive chemicals that collect in the liver when it metabolizes alcohol.

- Get more sleep if you can (in bed rather than on the bus or at your desk).

- Have a long soak in the bath and add some soothing oil. The steam will help to sweat out those nasty toxins.

- Go outside and get some fresh air, but stay out of the sun.

- Remember it won't last forever. You'll feel better the next day.

How Can I Avoid Another Hangover?

- Duh – don't drink.

- Duh – don't drink so much.

- Eat a good meal before you go out. A glass of milk can protect the stomach and slow down the absorption of alcohol.

- Don't mix your drinks too much. Stick to only red or white wine, beer or spirits.

- Have a non-alcoholic drink or two between each alcoholic one. Don't drink fizzy drinks – they actually increase the amount of alcohol that gets into the blood stream. Avoid red wine as it contains congeners that are thought to produce longer-lasting hangovers. And you don't want that, do you? Eat with your drinks.

- After the party, get some fresh air before going to bed. Drink plenty of water and take some Vitamin C before hitting the sack. If you haven't eaten all night, eat some toast. On second thoughts, eat some toast anyway.

| Technique | Tool | Wisdom | Cleaning | Chore |

Plant an Idea for the Bathroom

What colour are your fingers? Do they boast a hint of green or are they decidedly flesh-coloured? There is more to houseplant choice and care than you might think if yours are the latter. Let's take it from the top. Think of your home as a mini earth equipped with an entire range of different climates.

Your bathroom is humid, sometimes hot and steamy, and on some days rather tropical (if you don't ventilate properly). Certain plants just love these humid conditions. Try not to make your bathroom into a greenhouse, however. Do let some fresh air in from time to time or it will become green with mould rather than plants. Maidenhair and Boston ferns enjoy the conditions and certainly make the bathroom look more exotic, although ferns are not fans of too much direct light.

Aspidistras are low maintenance and orchids like humidity but do need diffused sunlight. Hang a Spider Plant in there to fill a large window. They are very low maintenance and therefore ideal on the plant housework front, too. The Peace Lily and

Chinese Evergreen (aglaonema) like medium light. In rooms with little light, the so-called 'bathroom plant' might be a good choice. Otherwise known as the Snake Plant or Mother-in-Law's tongue, it may be too much of a commitment, so try a trailing Philodendron instead. This plant is particularly good at cleansing the air so is a good choice for the bathroom.

If there is only one light source and you have a selection of plants, rotate them. Don't over-water (water less in winter) and put in unbreakable pots, particularly if you plan to hang them. You don't want accidents to happen and shards of dangerous ceramic or pot in the bath. Ouch. Avoid putting plants in hot or cold draughts.

Get Even Greener Fingers

Have a go at creating a mini ledge garden if conditions and size on your windowsill allow.

Put different plants in the same colour pots or the same plants in pots of contrasting hues. It's a great way to impress visitors – those who view the plants from outside and those who venture within. Be careful when you water them if you live in an apartment and ensure the pots are firmly secured. Neighbours may not appreciate a free shower in the morning or evening or a pot landing in their head. Don't use the pots as ashtrays.

Rule of Thumb

To detect when to water, press your thumb into the soil to test moisture content and only water when it feels dry. If the soil loses touch with the sides of the container, you left it rather late. To revive a dehydrated plant, loosen the top layer of soil to allow the water to permeate to the roots. Water the plant thoroughly and spray the leaves with tepid water.

Cleaning Leaves

Yes, houseplants involve housework, but not too much. Dust is dangerous. It not only spoils the appearance of your plant but it also blocks the leaf's pores and restricts its breathing. It blocks out light and may contain harmful chemicals. Hardy plants with glossy leaves can be cleaned by sponging the leaves with soapy water. Smaller plants need gentle treatment and should not be cleaned with liquid or chemicals. Use a soft brush to lightly dust the surface. Don't wash or polish young leaves.

Handle with Care

Watering is key to caring for your houseplant. Too much water and the root system will be unable to breathe, causing yellowed leaves, rot and death. Too little water and the plant will also die. Use tepid water for plant watering. The warmer the room, the greater the evaporation and the more water your plant will require.

Petiquette in the Bathroom

Those of you who have a pet will know that it offers unconditional love, non-judgemental companionship and unquestioning loyalty in return for a bowl of food twice a day, a quick romp in the park, regular brushing and a comfy place to sleep. Cats and dogs (and maybe even fish) are always delighted to see you. They are also good for your health according to Australian research that shows how pet owners are less at risk of heart disease and high blood pressure than non-owners. In addition, pets are known to boost spirits and relieve depression.

Pet Peeves

Mind Muddy Paws

If you have a carpeted bathroom, both you and it may fume if Rover comes in with muddy paws. Just in case he fancies a snoop in there and you can't prevent it, wipe his paws at the front or back door or invent shoes for dogs.

Loo Stop

If your pet does urinate on a carpeted bathroom floor, act immediately. Put paper towels over the stain and dab gently until most of the urine has been absorbed. You can then spray with your carpet cleaning liquid and blot again. You risk ruining the pile of the carpet if you rub energetically.

Hygiene Hazard

Dogs bring fleas and faeces and all sorts of nastiness into the house – the little critters hitch a ride on the back of animals as a form of cheap public transport and are exactly what you don't want in the bathroom. Keep this a bacteria-free zone. Vacuum the carpet regularly if Rover or Felix pop a paw inside. To freshen and deodorize a smelly bathroom carpet, sprinkle with bicarbonate of soda (with a handful of dried and crushed lavender flowers if you like), leave for a few minutes and then vacuum.

Helpful Hygiene

- Keep your bathroom a pet-free zone. Rubber ducks and other waterproof animals are fine, if you must. Never allow your cat or dog to urinate in the bathroom. Read on to find out what to do if they do do-do.
- Depending on the species and breed, your pet will need to be groomed and bathed from time to time. If you must do it in the bathroom, scrub and sanitize the bath thoroughly afterwards and use vet-approved shampoos. Don't share towels, soap or toothbrushes.
- If your dog does sneak into the bathroom and leave you an unpleasant message, chastise immediately, not later. He will not know why you are cross if you don't do it straight away.

Litter Alert
Litter boxes may be toilets for cats but they do not belong in the bathroom. Like the kitchen, this is a no-go (literally) zone for felines.

Store not Jaw
Put medication away safely to avoid pets thinking pills are new treats. Medication for human consumption can kill animals.

Fish Deserve Respect
A goldfish bowl is only a temporary home for Goldie – his or her (how do you tell?) permanent address should be a correct-sized aquarium complete with plants, a pump and toys, etc. Clean it once a month, don't overfeed Goldie and, if you use tap water, check if chemicals need to be added to remove the chlorine.

Toxic Plants
Do choose your houseplants with care – some are toxic. Cats like to dig in the soil and can be harmed by certain plants. Do some research or consult your vet.

Dust, Wipe and Vacuum
This tried and trusted trio plays a crucial role in households with pets. If you don't have time for them twice a week, perform them as often as you can.

Technique

Tool

Wisdom

Cleaning

Chore

Shortcuts

 Prepare to Score (On the Domestic Field)

Maximum score in minimum time. How does that sound? Tempting? Ten out of ten in ten minutes takes some beating, guys. Here's a set of Top Trump Tips. Go from hero to zero in no time at all.

10 Out of 10 in 10

1 Don't be a Mug

You can use a proper holder, a pretty mug or even a glass for keeping your toothbrushes upright (and together). Give the vessel itself a good clean every week (every fortnight at the most). Pop it in the dishwasher. Otherwise it could get all yucky at the bottom and provide ideal conditions for a bacteria experiment. Don't give homes to germs.

2 10 Over 10 with 10

Put some essential oil into your bath to relax or refresh. Add around 10 drops to a nice warm, but not too hot, bath. Try lavender to soothe, rosemary to revive. Add some rosehip oil to your moisturizer to soften lines. Massage your face in the bath with it. Almond oil is great for hands and dry, irritated faces. Argan oil is rich in vitamin E and a luxury massage oil.

3 Where's the M and M Party?

Mould and mildew are party animals that really get around, especially to those places they are not invited or wanted. They are particularly keen to hang around shower curtains. A good trick for evicting mildew is to cut a fresh lemon in half, dip in borax powder and then rub over the affected area on the curtain, bathroom tile or bath.

4 The M and M Party is Over

Bathrooms are humid environments and therefore particularly attractive for mould and mildew. Ventilate the room properly to discourage them forming, focusing on the area most prone to attack. M and M hate it when it's warm and dry. Try spraying affected zones with neat white vinegar, leaving for half an hour and then wiping off.

5 Playing Away

Public bathrooms, showers and loos are often not the most hygienic of places. Use them if you must but if you are particularly concerned about the level of cleanliness there are a few tricks to keep up your trouser leg. Avoid going barefoot in public showers unless you fancy a fresh dose of Athlete's foot. Use paper towels to turn taps on and off.

6 Green and Clean

Have a go at being greener in the bathroom by avoiding the use of chemicals. Pour boiling water and salt down a smelly drain rather than pumping it with bleach. Use tea tree oil to disinfect the loo, by adding a few drops to a jug of water, pouring it into the pan and leaving it for an hour or so. Freshen the bathroom with essential oil in a burner.

7 Sun, Sun and Sun

Hang your bath, hand and face towels in the sun on warm days – this helps keep them clean and dry between uses. No more musty smells and dirty looks (or dirty smells and musty looks). The sun is another pair of hands in the house. You will keep dust mites at bay and your towels will smell nicer, too. This is not a substitute for cleaning.

8 Floored in the Bathroom

If you have a carpeted bathroom, you need to take extra care to keep it clean, dry and free of stains. Vacuum regularly to keep dust mites at bay. Bathmats should be used always and laundered frequently in order to prevent the carpet becoming damp from your dripping feet, body or hair. Remove any stains immediately (don't eat or drink in the bathroom).

9 Gold Stars in the Bathroom

Parents use motivational charts in the bathroom to encourage their children to learn how to use the potty or loo, clean their teeth and hair and learn the principles of hygiene. It is not a bad idea for some adults. If your housemate or partner need similar encouragement why not make a chart and give them a special treat for cleaning the loo.

10 Bathroom Budget

If you are saving money, try one or more of the following tricks. Use leftover cheap shampoo as handwash – just decant it into a posh empty bottle. Use old toothbrushes to clean shoes or scrub tricky crevices. Mix freebie scents with some cheap baby oil and use as a bath oil. Dilute expensive bubble bath, often concentrated, and shampoo.

| Technique | Tool | Wisdom | Cleaning | Chore |

Do it Together

It is true that a problem shared is a problem halved. It applies within relationships and within the home. Give your relationship 100 per cent. Put in your 50 per cent. It's a simple equation. What other deal would give you that sort of return?

It is reasonable for one partner to expect the other to do their share of the household tasks. Share the chores and share the joys. Partnerships work better when respect and care are involved. Always being the one to load the dishwasher or do the washing up is not going to make you feel respected and cared for. It's another quite simple equation. It may make you feel resentful and upset, taken for granted. That is not good for relationships, romantic or platonic.

We have established that housework keeps you healthy, brings rewards, spices up your love life and makes you more attractive. Divide and drool. Don't just talk about it – it's Chore, Chore not Jaw, Jaw.

Why not draw up a list of the household tasks that need doing and work out who does what, who hates what, who doesn't mind what? Too big an ask? Too much like

Domestic God says ...

If you know your partner really dislikes one particular job, put L or DM. That's compromise. Uh-oh another 'C' word.

hard work? OK, guys, here it is, all done and dusted (well, actually you have to do that bit...)

Photocopy the page and then fill in the boxes as follows – one of you uses the photocopied page (don't argue now!):

L = Like
H = Hate
DM = Don't Mind

Have a look at the completed charts and share the chores so that you have equal amounts of dislikes and likes (no cheating now, guys). Do deals on the Don't Minds. Add any jobs that are missing and apply to your particular circumstances. This exercise is part of the whole process of domestic democracy. Don't start the Chore Wars – be a Domestic Diplomat and do your bit for world peace.

Dirty Devil says ...

If you know your partner really likes one particular job, you may be tempted to put RL against it. That's naughty!

Domestic Democracy

Chore	Like	Hate	Don't Mind
DUSTING			
VACUUMING			
POLISHING			
TIDYING UP			
WIPING SURFACES			
CLEANING THE BATH			
CLEANING THE SHOWER			
CLEANING THE SINK			
WASHING OUT THE BIDET			
PUTTING STUFF IN THE CUPBOARDS			
HANGING UP CLOTHES			
SORTING DIRTY CLOTHES			
DEALING WITH DRY CLEANING			
WASHING THE TILES			
TIDYING DRAWERS			
CLEANING THE LOO			
CHANGING THE LOO ROLL			
WASHING THE FLOOR			
EMPTYING THE TRASH BIN			
WASHING THE WALLS			
WASHING WINDOWS			
REPLENISHING SUPPLIES			
PUTTING LIDS BACK ON BOTTLES			
SWEEPING THE FLOOR			
CLEANING THE WINDOWS			
CLEANING BLINDS			
WASHING CURTAINS			
REPLACING BULBS			
CHANGING PLUGS			
CARING FOR PLANTS			
RECYCLING			

Wise Dude Mess Mantra

You will know that clutter has reached dangerous levels when you fall over your dirty socks in the bathroom, slide on a bar of soap on the floor, get concussion when you open the cabinet or can't locate your razor among the mess on the surface.

Cut the Clutter

Everything we bring through our front door needs a storage place, either temporary or permanent, or a place in the trash, so here's how to deal with most of the stuff.

Uncontrolled collecting, unnecessary hoarding and sheer laziness when it comes to containing piles of stuff are all enemies of a tidy house.

Remember that the bathroom is the smallest room in the house, generally speaking, and that packaging, cosmetics, lotions and potions should be kept to a minimum. Each and every item you put in the bathroom will need attention – you will have to keep it tidy, clean, yuk-free and current. It will need a home. Think of all the lids you will have to put back on! Keep reading matter to an absolute minimum and keep it clean (metaphorically and physically. You never know what age your guests may be – you don't want to frighten children with your loo literature, do you? So chaps, gather your loincloths, make the decision to clear the clutter, embark upon the mission

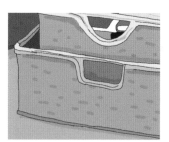

and divide things into the Need and Don't Need piles.

Everything in the Need pile should be found a home. Build a cabinet or some extra shelves for the Daily Need pile and put the rest in a plastic storage container, safe from prying eyes and curious jaws. Ask yourself why you are keeping some of the stuff. Sentimental attachment to bathroom equipment is not really a valid answer, guys.

Bye Bye Clutter Bunnies

Will you ever wear that cologne your first love gave you? Has it not gone slightly sour rather like your relationship? Suncream has a shelf life so don't keep it season after season. Old razors get rusty and lose their edge. Soggy nail files are pointless. Batteries rust and perish. Saving small slivers of soap is not a good idea. Melt and make into a new one or chuck. Recycling old toothbrushes is fine, but put them with the cleaning equipment or you/your housemate may get a mouthful. Put treats for guests in a small plastic container marked Guests (duh!) – spare toothbrush, razor, hotel giveaway soap, freebie cologne or scent, spare shampoo and conditioner. Make up an emergency wash bag for yourself – it could live in your suitcase. Sort and store. Be ruthless, make it roofless. Don't apply to relationships – with humans or pets.

Safe Disposal

If you are throwing medicine away, always remember to dispose of it safely. Check what your local regulations dictate first. Generally speaking you can pour liquid medicine down the drain or loo and it is best to put solids in a bin liner and then in the trash. Tie safely and if contents include pills or solid medicines, remove from your home immediately (not just as far as the trash, lazy), keeping it safe from children or animals. Ask your local pharmacy for advice if you are not sure what to do. If you want to get rid of leftover bleach, for example, pour it down the drain but in small quantities and never with another substance. It may react dangerously with it.

Need, Don't Need

Use this mantra when you are about to tackle the mess:

D OMESTIC
E NERGY
C AN
L IBERATE
U
T OTALLY.
T IDY
E VERY
R OOM **C** LEAR
        I T
        A WAY **A** LL
               G UYS
               E VENTUALLY
               N EED
               T IDINESS

- Keep a container for instant tidy-ups when your mother visits – log baskets, crates on castors, cardboard storage boxes can all be quickly filled and hidden in the spare room.

QED → QAD

QED (*Quod erat demonstrandum*) – people say and read this Latin expression every day (OK, every now and then). 'That which was to be demonstrated' – posh for proof is in the pudding and we've got the pudding now (for those not in the know yet). Well, in this case, it is QAD (*Question, Answer, Danger*) or watch out 'cos the pudding might be poisoned. The Danger could be a Beware Bacteria, an

Q	A	D
My partner keeps telling me to put the lid down on the loo? Is it really a problem to leave it up?	Yes. Always put the loo lid down, particularly when you have used cleaning agents.	Germs and particles of cleaning liquid can leap out of the loo and splash anything within jumping distance. Loo brush or toothbrush?
I sometimes borrow my housemate's towel and it does not go down well. Is this really a yelling issue?	Yes. Don't share towels, particularly if you or your housemate is unwell.	You will be sharing towels, bacteria and infections. Beware Bacteria!
My new partner says my bathroom stinks. It looks clean enough. Is it a problem?	Yes – you obviously need to clean your bathroom equipment. You may have a mouldy shower curtain, a dirty loo or a blocked drain.	Bathrooms are bacterial experiments waiting to happen. Cross-contamination is a major risk in this room. Be extra hygienic.
I would like to put candles all round the bath and make it all romantic for my partner. Is there any problem with this?	Yes, make sure you use non-flammable candle holders and don't leave the room with the candles lit for even one minute.	Lit candles left unsupervised are a major fire risk. Don't leave the room. Don't leave the matches for children to use later.

Amoeba Alert, an early E-Coli warning. It might just be a stink bomb siren. It gets easier once you've read a few, promise. The idea is to alert you to the perils that lurk in the bathroom – the domestic dangers waiting to pounce on a daily basis, probably without you even having the slightest notion of their existence. Brief yourself before de-briefing yourself. You know it makes sense.

Q	A	D
I always put my towel on the loo seat while I am having a shower. My new partner freaked out when I did this? Who is right?	Your new partner is right – looks like you will be establishing a more hygiene bathroom routine!	The towel could easily become contaminated with surface germs. Beware Bacteria!
My cat's litter tray is in the bathroom. Is this dangerous?	Yes. The bathroom needs to be as hygienic as possible and keep the tray in there is not helping to create a bacteria-free zone.	Litter trays should not be in kitchens, bathrooms, bedrooms or living areas. They are smelly and full of potentially hazardous germs.
I want to dry my hair in the bathroom – why can't I just get a plug put in?	Electricity and water do not go together – no plugs should be in the bathroom (except special shaving or toothbrush ones).	Do not use electrical appliances near water. Never submerge them in the water. You could electrocute yourself.
I bought my toothbrush on my summer holiday last year. Should I get another now I am about to go on my annual holiday again?	You should see your dentist and hygienist immediately and learn some basic facts about oral hygiene. Buy a sturdy toothbrush today.	Your teeth, gums, breath and social life are at risk if you don't floss and clean regularly, using a proper toothbrush.

| Technique | Tool | Wisdom | Cleaning | Chore |

A Miscellany of Domestic Wisdom

This page is for dipping into whenever you feel the need for words of wisdom, for whatever reason, whether to motivate yourself or your partner, impress your in-laws or outlaws, chat up a new acquaintance, liven up conversation at a dull dinner or simply amuse yourself in bed. Unlike food at a party, double-dipping is safe. Think of it as a fondue of wisdom, free for all to dip in and out of and back again (not too cheesy?).

Wisdom from the Man and Woman in the Street

If a man is loved for all seasons, personal hygiene will be one of the reasons.
David Barbour

If a man gets the bathroom fresh, he might be next.
Stan Moller

If a man's home is his castle, his bathroom may be the moat and his cellar the dungeon, but his bedroom does not have to be the torture chamber and his kitchen the stable.
Arthur Holmes

Domestic Dynamics

Activity	Level of effort	Calories burned
WASHING THE BATH	MEDIUM	50
WIPING SURFACES	LIGHT	40
WASHING TILES	MEDIUM	90
TIDYING BATHROOM	MEDIUM	30

Bathroom Safe, Bathroom Wise

Don't eat in the bathroom unless you really have to munch on toast while shaving. Clear up after yourself or bacteria will enjoy the leftovers. Bacteria party in the bathroom – don't provide the hors d'oeuvres for free.

Open the windows after a particularly steamy bath or shower. You might want to instal an extractor fan. All the moisture and humidity will encourage mould and mildew. Keep it cool.

If you have a tiled bathroom, wipe the tiles clean regularly with an all-purpose non-scratch cleaning liquid.

What you see is not what you get with dust mites. They are invisible. For something so small, they wreak huge havoc, particularly with those prone to allergic attacks or asthma. Just to give you an idea, half a teaspoon of house dust contains around one thousand dust mites and unspeakable quantities of faeces. There are dust mites in the bathroom too, munching merrily on our dead skin, swilled down with a dash of Perspiration Nouveau. It is the protein in the shed skin casts that triggers the asthma problems. Keep it clean, guys.

Wisdometer

- Check battery-operated smoke alarms weekly and electric ones every month. Replace batteries twice a year. Put it on the chore chart. Keep the grille of the smoke detector clean, too.

- Always check the manufacturer's instructions on equipment. Booklets are included for a purpose. Nota Bene, mate, or buy a Latin Dictionary. Check how to use a fire extinguisher and where plus how to install, test, use and maintain.

- Always check safety instructions for electrical equipment and keep the literature in one safe place – emergency phone numbers, leaflets and guarantees.

- Always check that plugs and leads are not near heat, flame or water.

Index

Do You Know It All Already?

QUIZ ANSWERS

HOW OFTEN SHOULD YOU CLEAN THE BATH?
A

WHY LIGHT A MATCH IN THE BATHROOM?
B

DO YOU DISINFECT YOUR LOO BRUSH?
A

WHY IS IT IMPORTANT TO KEEP THE TOILET LID DOWN?
C AND E

WHY SHOULD YOU REMOVE DUST REGULARLY FROM SURFACES?
C

WHEN DID YOU LAST EMPTY THE LOO BIN?
C

DO YOU BATHE WITH YOUR DOG?
B

LOOK AT YOUR BATHROOM FLOOR. WHAT DO YOU SEE?
B

HOW OFTEN SHOULD YOU WASH YOUR BATH MAT?
D

WHY DO YOU NEED TO VENTILATE THE BATHROOM?
A